C000084039

SPARKS

Norah Hanson was born in Hull, in 1937, and has been a proud resident ever since. She spent her working life teaching in secondary schools, then turned to writing after her retirement in 1996. Widowed in 1994, she is nonetheless not short of company – she has six children, seventeen grandchildren and six great-grandchildren.

Her poetry has been shortlisted for the Bridport Prize, featured on BBC Radio 4, and published in numerous magazines and anthologies. She is the author of three collections of poetry, including *Love Letters & Children's Drawings* (2011) and *Under a Holderness Sky* (2013), both published by Valley Press.

Sparks

Norah Hanson

Valley Press

First published in 2016 by Valley Press
Woodend, The Crescent, Scarborough, YO11 2PW
www.valleypressuk.com

ISBN 978-1-908853-76-9
Cat. no. VP0093

A CIP record for this book is available from the British Library.

Cover and text design by Jamie McGarry.

Supported using public funding by

ARTS COUNCIL
ENGLAND

LOTTERY FUNDED

Contents

Always for you, Harry

This Earth

Whether there is a God or not, the beauty
and music of this Earth merit a genuflection.
When the wind plays in the leaves of the
poplar at twilight and I hear the chatter,
I am blessed.

When I arrive home after an absence to find
pink chrysanthemum growing on a yellow-
starred carpet of green and a plethora of white
roses sprawled over the roof of the garden shed,
I am blessed.

I will be sorry to leave this world.

I am grateful that my eyes can look on its
beauty, my nose can inhale the scents of
summer, my ears can listen to birdsong
at dawn, my fingers can touch the silk of
leaves when my feet take me walking in
the forest.

Whether there is a God or not,
I stand in awe, in my own body,
in my given time and space.
The beauty and music of this Earth
merit a genuflection.

Manna From Heaven

The sky at night dropped stuff. That's how she came
to be wearing a designer dress and hat, diamonds
on her fingers, a gold pendant around her neck.
When questioned by the police, who arrested
her for disturbing the peace in the marketplace,
she assured them she was not high on drugs or drink,
but filled with the Holy Spirit. God had blessed her,
just as he had the Israelites wandering in the desert
when he caused manna to rain from heaven.

God had seen her predicament as she pushed all
her worldly possessions in a supermarket trolley
to her preferred park bench behind the bushes.
She had supped from a small bottle of whiskey
she found in her trolley, said her night prayers
and drifted to sleep under the stars.

On waking, she had found the hat and dress draped
over the bushes, the diamond ring and gold pendant
glinting on the path in the rays of the morning sun.
Of course she questioned her vision, rubbed her eyes
once or twice, but there they were for sure, just like the
presents left by Santa when she was a child, when she
once was loved and had been able to like herself, before
the bombs dropped and she found herself orphaned.

So why shouldn't the sky drop stuff into the bushes
while she slept? Why shouldn't she remember what
it was like to be loved? Why shouldn't she stand in
the marketplace and thank God for her good fortune?

Imprint

A snapshot moment, startling as an
after-image on Hiroshima's walls.
Shopping for Christmas bargains,
pushing my babies in a second-hand
pram, their hands in mittens made
from the sleeve ends of old jumpers,
they were blanketed against winter,
safe in my keeping, bonny and healthy.

I saw a crazed, dishevelled man with
no shoes, no coat, ragged trousers, snow
settling on his bare head and beard, tears
on his face. I knew him as some mother's
son. He remained imprinted on my retina;
until years later I embraced him.

Walking Alone

I am walking alone, one foot
in front of the other, between
yellow gorse growing beside
the disused railway track.
I meet couples and families,
the odd dog that sniffs my hand.
The last time I walked this path
I walked with you and our kids
were young and scampering.

We had Granny with us that day.
We left her on a bench, raced
down the cliff to fossil-crusted
shores and crashing waves.

Freckles had time to sprout
before we began the climb up;
treasures in backpacks, kids
salt-sprayed, parched, fretful.

We found Granny in a cafe,
drinking tea and eating cake.
We bought ice cream and
walked back on the old
railway track between the
yellow gorse as the sun set.

I walk alone now, all my dead
resting under my ribs, my living
lodged in my heart.

Spark

I wouldn't mind another crack at this life business.
When the light dims in my eyes and the river of my
blood becomes stagnant, I would hope that the spark
which danced in the spaces between the solid matter
of my body would not be extinguished, but leave with
the last breath I exhaled to birth again in a quickening
embryo or a dormant seed.

I've wondered how it feels to be a seagull, soaring
on thermals rising from the ocean; or to be supple
as a vulture, able to bend my neck into the shoulder-
blade of my wing and rest awhile, before instinct
triggers me to find meat to tear from a carcass
which once housed the spark dancing inside a lion
or a gazelle.

I've wondered how it feels to be a racehorse – heart
drumming in my chest, nostrils dilated, snorting
hot breath, the spur of a whip on my flanks, hooves
thundering on turf – or a fish; would I miss my arms
and fingers, would I be aware of their absence?
Could I become the life force silver-shimmering
in a green blade of grass?

I've wondered most of all how it feels to be gifted
with such talent that the spark within you ignites,
causing your soul to sing, your limbs to dance
and poetry to be written in the spaces between
your moving, so that all who hear and watch you
are blessed. I wouldn't mind another crack at
this life business.

A New Song to Sing

The parents embraced their young
sons, before they were given a horse
to ride into the wilderness of the hills
and wait for the spirit to speak their
new name and give them their
own song to sing.

When they returned to the camp
where the fires smoked and the
people called the river brother
and the gentle breeze sister,
the elders looked deep into their
eyes, placed a blessing hand
on their head and clothed them
in the garments of the brave.

Would that I could have sent
my own sons into the wilderness
to find the spirit they vainly
sought in the noise of the city.

Let Me Hear You Again

Speak to me as you did when your
mind, lips and tongue connected
to speak your first word and I was
blessed to receive your greeting.

Let me hear again the roar of your
laughter, the shout of your joy, your
quick response to banter, the protest
songs you sang in your youth.

Loosen your tongue, open your throat.
Howl, if you must.
I will hear you as I did when your first
word sprang into the space between us.

The Music of My Life

Music and lyrics have always been in my life.
Lullabies, nursery rhymes, the haunting refrain of
'Tantum ergo' when the monstrance was held up
at Benediction. 'Family favourites' on the radio,
my Granny singing Irish ballads and rebel songs
when she was in her cups. Hollywood musicals
when I dreamed of meeting my own 'Secret Love'.

'It's a zither melody' as we walked in crocodile
back to school from the sports field, and the joy
of music lessons with Miss McGee when we
sang 'Barbara Allan' and 'The Oak and the Ash',
lyrics imprinted in my mind. My father's cornet,
the music of the brass bands, playing the piano
and singing for him before he died, 'O My Papa'.

Learning to play Mozart on the piano at College.
The ecstasy of the chords which spurted saliva
into my mouth and sent me hurrying home to you.
The voice of Pavarotti, 'Nessun Dorma' when
your nights were full of pain and Enya singing
'I dreamt I dwelt in marble halls' the day you died
and I wanted you to love me still the same.

Our son in his youth, with his long curly hair,
beard and guitar, 'Hey Mr. Tambourine Man'
and 'Stay forever young', before fate robbed
him of his daring.

Still the music plays and they sing their dreams
in harmony, my young girls with their lives
before them. They dance to the rhythm of today,
setting the pace for the journey into tomorrow.
In the spaces between the notes, in the pregnant
waiting for all that is yet to come, I hear the echo
of the music of my life, the glory, the sorrow, the
joy, the longing for you to love me still the same.

Homecoming

Dark clouds weep a storm outside.
I listen to the gulping gurgle of
water in the drainpipe. The brown
of the fence is darkening, tree
branches stoop, not a bird in sight.

Rose petals have spilled summer
onto the clutter of my kitchen table.
A Christmas cactus has come into
its own, flaunting red flowers at
the tips of fat shiny green leaves.

Yesterday, it was a miserable spiky
insignificant thing, sad and tired
as grief; lonely as the long years
I've spent without you, building
a path out of pain and sorrow.

Today, as the dark clouds weep a
storm outside, I have arrived back
into myself, to find you here in the
warmth of my kitchen, where the
Christmas cactus blooms again.

Multi-tasking

Naked, dealing with my morning ablutions,
the soap slithers out of my hand. I bend to
retrieve it, see fluff and dust on the U-bend,
stretch my arm over the bowl to reach
a cleaning cloth, wipe the left-hand side
of the bend, realise my arm is not rubbery
enough to tackle the other side and try
to stand up. I can't. I'm stuck.

The only way out of the confined space I've
trapped myself in is to slither backwards.
Face down, bum up, I lean on my lower
arms, wriggle until my upper body is free,
kneel up and crack my temple on the flush
handle of the toilet. When the room stops
spinning, I totter to my bedroom, crawl under
the duvet and wait for the throbbing to abate.

And that, I tell the guests at the reception,
is why I have a black eye. I am not, as my
dear departed friend might have said, trying
to upstage her at her own funeral.

Tradition

You can establish tradition
anywhere, in anyone's house,
in your local pub, in church,
on a park bench, in a café.
Once your bottom has warmed
a seat on a regular basis, it
traditionally becomes yours.
If someone else sits there,
they fidget when you arrive,
move to another place or leave.

Not so long ago, a new tradition,
more in keeping with Christmas
nowadays, became established.
Gospel readings were replaced
with bulletins from fantastic
families with fantastic kids
who achieved fantastic things,
went on fantastic holidays to
ski resorts and warm climes,
while the rest of us avoided
eye contact with our bank
managers and endured the angst
of dysfunctional family life.

Now we hang plastic holly wreaths,
not the prickly crown of thorns dropping
blood-red berries. Christmas starts before
November, and is over by Boxing Day.
Who needs twelve days or twelve apostles
when we can have late night shopping,
instant credit, and satisfied kids playing
on computer games as we sleep off our
hangovers?

No matter that the ancient story of
a refugee mother birthing her child
in unhygienic conditions still happens.
Such kids come to a bad end anyway.

Northerners

Christmas Eve, I am travelling with
Northerners on the train to Edinburgh.
They smile, talk in loud voices, laugh
frequently, help lift my case, offer me
a drink as the train races along the east
coast. The sky above Lindisfarne is
ablaze and I think the seals will be
singing a lament to the dying of the day.

A young girl with a sweet voice starts
to sing 'Silent Night'. A raucous female
voice joins in. A fat fellow stops
talking football, grins at me, stands up
to conduct the chorus of voices joining
the choir. His signal tempers the voice
of the loud female to a surprisingly
beautiful contralto.

We sing as the light fades from the sky.
'Silent Night', reverently rendered, is
followed by 'Jingle Bells', 'Rudolph
the Red-nosed Reindeer' and a 'Twelve
Days of Christmas' where the gifts given
are a wee bit naughty. The laughs
are loud and the quips come thick
and fast.

I like Northerners. They know how
to make an old girl feel young again.

Targeted

Winter 2010

A shivering mouse came in from the cold
and took up residence in a kitchen cupboard.
Gutters buckled under the weight of snow,
hung perilously down the outside walls.
Unable to dig out my car, I fell flat on
my back trying to skate to the shops.

A fierce cold and spluttering cough caused
me to wet my knickers. Confined indoors,
I developed cabin fever. My landline cut off,
my mobile inexplicably went to silent mode,
my wireless refused to tune to Radio 4. My email
was hacked, my address book stolen and friends
were asked to send $2000 dollars to rescue
me from Malaysia where I had been mugged
and robbed of my passport and possessions.

I became convinced that something out there
in cyberspace was targeting me. I did see
strange lights in the sky which my son told me
were flying saucers. I was willing to be abducted
for a while, but thought it plain mean to just
have fun with me. Some people would really
crack up and require sectioning. I did get to
the stage where I was screaming 'Bring it on,
why don't you?!' It stopped for a while,
then came back with a vengeance.

Light bulbs shattered, fuses blew; the door-
bell rang constantly as people checked on my
continuing existence. Today, a Christian bloke
who thinks he has a vocation to visit the sick called
round. He stayed two hours, ate all my Christmas
chocolates and told me he was doing me a favour
as I am diabetic and he knows about these things.
He said he will return.

I have taken the batteries out of the door-bell,
but he has strong fists. His knock can wake
the dead. If he thinks I am dead, he'll probably
kick the door down. I have resolved to greet
him with a Christian kiss next time he calls,
and pray that he will catch all of my germs,
including the ones from outer space which
have been making my life a misery.

Winter Evening

6th January 2011

The room is warm, the taste of chocolate lingers
on my palate. If I were a dog or a child, I would
lie on the rug and sleep in front of the fire. Poets
are gathered here, pens move across paper. I am
searching for inspiration. My tea cools in a mug
painted with the stalks and trumpet-heads of lilies.

How little attention I pay to the craft of designers.
The cloth covering the table is a white-laced web
of flowers, an unbroken symmetry. She gave me
a satsuma for my cold. I am creating an abstract
sculpture of peel, pips and tissues on her carpet.
Think it may have a random chance of success.

My sniffs and coughs are loud in the silence of
this room. Outside, revellers spill from pubs,
drivers in warm cars suck boiled sweets, listen
to music, carry wallets, mobile phones and house
keys. Headlights shine on people in shop doorways,
huddled in sleeping bags lined with newspaper.

The room is warm, the taste of chocolate lingers
on my palate. It is the feast of the Epiphany and
tonight a child will cry, a woman weep, a man howl.
Someone will love beyond endurance. I cannot
see, I cannot hear. My abstract sculpture has
grown. I must flush it down the toilet.

No Herald to the Dawn

It is the long lonely time of dark days
when birds stay in nests and there is no
herald to the dawn. Your absence fills
this house. The glitter of lighted green
trees is past. Money has bled from bank
accounts, the boiler gobbles energy, bills
soar and hearses carry the dead to graves.

I will go to the woods, find snowdrops
in wet earth and swellings on the tips of
branches. I will speak into the mist until
I conjure your response and when the sun
lights my way, I will walk to the tearoom
where you and I spoke of this and that
and you and me when we were young.

Sparks in the Night Sky

No apple bough or Fern Hill of Dylan's
childhood haunts, but a terraced house
in a concrete street and broken bombed
buildings. I played my dreams, 'kiss catch'
with boys round the Victory bonfire which
shot sparks into the night sky.

I built an altar from the rubble inside the
skeleton of a church, picked gold dandelions
to stand in jam jars, fashioned a cross from
splintered wood, made the sign of the cross
and knelt to sing my prayer to a God who'd
saved us from the Nazis.

Wakened each morning by my father's
step on the stairs, I followed him to
sit at the table as he slurped hot tea
from a pint mug before coughing
and spitting into the fire my mother
had coaxed to life.

I savoured the sound of their quiet
voices, and the touch of his hand
on my head before he left for work.

No apple bough, no fields, but sparks
flying in the night sky; a splintered
wooden cross, an altar made from
the rubble inside the skeleton of
church, golden dandelions in jam jars,
and the touch of his hand on my head.

Hessle Foreshore

Slate sheen on river mud,
infant green-haired rocks
and the arc of the bridge
spanning the Humber.
I walked here in my teens,
stood in pelting rain when
thunder crashed and jagged
silver forks crackled light
in the sky.

New build now where the
farmer lived. I had to duck
to pass between two sties
housing a huge boar and sow.
They scared the life out of me.

The farmer ladled milk, warm
from the cow, into my tin jug.
I'd call Tommy, his chestnut
horse, to gallop to the fence
and eat grass from my palm.

A rotting beached boat, games
of pirates and rescued maidens,
flat stones to plop over the water
and tennis on the court of the big
house when the family was away.

Silverfish scuttled in the hearth
of the cottage my friend lived in.
It has solar panels on the roof now,
double glazing, white pebble dash,
a hanging basket and a seat outside.

Gone the damp mustiness and the
pungent smell of her father's pipe
tobacco. Gone the fantasies of my
dreams, the unknown future and
the untended gardens of my youth.

Seasons

Sun-worshippers follow migrating birds south,
sip wine under parasols, lie naked on hot sand.
My skin needs the whip of an October breeze.
My eyes need to be unshaded to fill my irises
with the lushness of purple black brambles.
I savour the days when I can hang washing to
dry in my garden, before the coming of short
dark cold days. I watch sheets billow, towels
whip-crack, shirts flex arms and expand their
chests and long johns kick-dance in the wind.

Let me know English seasons, spiders' webs
bejewelled in the early morning, plums ripe
and succulent on trees, conkers bursting out
of prickly green cases. I will bury my dreams
beneath hard clay, wait for snowdrops to reach
for light. I will wake in my warm bed when
rain lashes the window and dawn comes late.

When the helmets of snowdrops shrink, I will
crawl on hands and knees, clearing leaf-mould
from my garden to find green blades of daffodil
erect with promise. Birds will steal moss from
hanging baskets. Bold, brassy and beautiful
dandelions will sprout in roadside verges, lawns,
flower beds and cracks in concrete. Children
will make wishes as they blow off the white
seeds. I will fill my nostrils with the scent of
lilac, cherry blossom and newly-cut grass.

When the pollen count is high, I will walk
where the sea washes my feet, feel my skin
cook gently in the heat. In the evening I will
cut roses to stand in a vase and let the fallen
petals be a pool of silk on my kitchen table.
I will sit in my garden until the sun sets, wake
early in my bed when dawn breaks, watch swans
glide in lakes, goldfinch flit in trees and freckles
sprout on the faces of my grandchildren.

When the birds gather in flocks and practise
for the marathon journey south, I will savour
the smell of bonfires and the gust of a fresh
autumn wind billowing the washing pegged
in my garden. I will gather brambles, bake
pies, light a fire in the evening, wake in my
warm bed when the rain lashes at the window
and dawn comes late.

Buns

I blame the buns, beckoning
behind the glass wall of the
counter in the baker's shop.
Pastry cases with strawberries
floating in red jelly, chocolate
éclairs, jam and lemon tarts,
cupcakes, cookies, iced buns,
and a whole array of creamy
delights.

I came in for a healthy brown
seeded loaf, tried to avert
my eyes from the sensuous
blatant display, handed over
my money and heard a voice,
unbidden, speaking from my
mouth, '*and a strawberry tart,
cupcake, and chocolate éclair
please*'.

I blame the buns. They should
be kept out of sight, under lock
and key, like illicit liquor in
speakeasies or tobacco in
supermarkets. There should
be a red light area where they
could ply their trade to sugar
addicts. They should not be
allowed in bread shops.

Grow Old Disgracefully

Make your morning prayer the sign
of the cross, and give two fingers
to the stuff which weighs you down.
Light up under a 'no smoking' sign.
Sit outside the Cathedral where the
down-and-outs gather and treat them
to a cup of tea and a beef burger.

Drink two cups of peppermint tea
after Christmas dinner and don't
be embarrassed by your windy
emissions. Be grateful for washing
machines, dishwashers, vacuum cleaners,
light bulbs, microwaves, electric kettles,
your senior citizen bus pass, false
teeth, spectacles, thermal underwear,
bed socks, slippers, hot water bottles,
duvets, clean sheets, colour television,
music centres, radio, hot dinners, cups
of tea, mobile phones, internet, hair dye,
legs which can still walk, hands you
can hold, chubby babies you can cuddle,
friends you can talk to and family you
can love and worry about.

Do something you have always dreamed
of doing but never thought you would.
Talk to foreigners, learn to say 'hello' in
their language. Walk in unfamiliar places,
get lost and ask someone to point you to
the nearest café. Sit at an occupied table
and start a conversation with strangers.

Go up in a hot air balloon. Engage cold
callers in conversation until you bore them
with the trivia of your life and they slam
the phone down on you. Rage against
bureaucracy. Shoot water pistols at your
grandchildren. Take them to the fair,
ride with them on dodgem cars, buy them
chips, toffee apples, ice creams, candy floss
and fizzy drinks. When they feel sick take
them home to their parents. Turn the tables
on your kids; strategically place your half-
drunk cup of coffee on the floor of their
living room so that someone can kick it
over. Always tell them you love them
and hug them before you leave.

Grafters

They come into your life, naked,
vulnerable, a mighty force you
have no defence against. They
cry you to attention, graft their
desires on your heart, take sleep
and reason from you and cast
a spell on you which you can't
or won't break.

They strengthen their hold with
every passing year, grafting their
joys and sorrows onto the throbbing
pulse of your life, and their children,
and *their* children, graft on the grafts
of generations until your heart's skin
is patched and stretched and aching
with the love and hurt they bring you.

Scruffs

Two suited store workers march the tousle-
haired scruff in baggy jogging bottoms and torn
sweatshirt out of the store onto the street,
where a wind is blowing and rain bounces
off the pavement. Another scruff squats,
back to the wall, under the awning of a shop.
I hurry past him, plastic bags full of food.
I don't want to think of the flotsam of young
men on our streets. I want to sleep soundly
in my bed each night.

Elmstead Wood

A few miles south of London Bridge,
beyond the traffic roar, the scurrying
surge of humanity, information flashing
on and off on electronic noticeboards,
the tinny Tannoy voice announcing
cancelled trains, I got off at the wrong
station onto a deserted platform and
heard birdsong in Elmstead Wood.

The world stilled as I waited on a
wooden bench for a train to take me
two stops down the line. Sunlight
danced in green foliage on a bank
of trees. Sudden the peace, long
the moment, surprising the joy on
the day you left us and I heard
the birds sing in Elmstead Wood.

In the Silence

Social chit-chat, loud music,
muted melody of booting
computers, keyboard thumps,
roar of traffic, strident shriek
of phones, alarms, fire engines
and ambulances; panic and fear
in voices from war zones where
bombs blast, gun shot crackles,
widows weep, children cry,
desperate people seek safety
on foreign soil and battle-weary
wounded soldiers are brought
home to listen to politicians
argue, harangue and theorise.

In the silence of their stopping,
in the unguarded moment,
in the gaze of a lover,
in the touch of your hand,
in the recognition of a stranger,
in the space between the notes,
in the quiet hours of the night,
in the journey from then to now,
in the leaving of yesterday,
in the waiting on an infant's cry,
in the stillness, in the aloneness,
I hear your voice.
I feel your presence.

Travelling

I travel through the spaces between us.
In my handbag is my passport, airline
tickets, tissues, a spare pair of knickers
in case I sneeze, mobile phone, loose
change for a coffee stop, spectacles,
a book, pen, foreign currency in my
purse, sterling safe in a separate wallet.

I travel through the spaces between us,
carrying your loss, my anxiety, our sorrow,
his hope, her ending. I carry the dreams
I once dreamed with you when the future
was distant and the path untrodden.

The Dance of the Kitchen

You switch on the kettle. I open the oven door
to check the casserole. She takes milk out of
the fridge, side-steps to avoid children racing
to the back door, hands you the milk, you put
tea bags and coffee granules into cups, pour on
hot water and milk, sprinkle sugar or sweeteners
carefully, calculating individual recipes. We blow
on the steam as we sip, swallow and chat.

A child dances in from the hall, showing off her
newly-acquired ability to point her toes and kick
her legs in the air. We pull in our stomachs, step
out of her way. Nursing a hangover, her cousin
blunders into the room in search of paracetamol.
I point him to a cupboard, you make him a coffee.
He grunts his thanks, makes his way back to bed.
You collect empty cups, leave them in the sink.
She scowls, puts on her apron, rolls up her sleeves
splatters and clatters as she washes up. The dancing
child comes back. You scoop her up, waltz her out
of the kitchen. She clears the table, puts out cutlery.
You return, reach into the cupboard for plates. I open
the oven door. She puts a chopping board on the
table for the steaming casserole to sit on. Leading
her cousins like a pied piper, the child returns.
All find a seat, all talk at once. I spoon food onto
plates, talk stops. The morning dance of the kitchen
is over. Act two will follow after pudding.

The Breeze

The breeze through the window carries
a perfume; rank in the evening, heavy
as a tear drop, intoxicating, pungent
of air and earth, a bursting sorrowful
longing, a menstrual outpouring.

I breathe its potency, drift into sleep.
It departs to return in the morning,
fresh green as cut grass; a gentle sigh,
full of promise, cool, pure, kissing my
face, sweet as the breath of a child.

Song Lines

We said farewell as the sun shone bright
in the blue Brisbane sky. Black, grey, white
clouds shift and reform as my plane climbs
above the ocean.

My head is full of musings and absences,
shifting, reforming, changing, like the song
lines sung to map this land from generation
to generation.

From the land of your birth, pilots have flown
me over continents, navigating lines drawn
on aeronautical charts, bringing me to your
wedding day,

the fruits of your union. Your sons grown
tall now, I come again and again to wonder at
the beauty of this land, hold in memory transient
moments of your life.

Clouds shift and reform. Seconds, minutes, hours
pass. Days come and go. I can never be here and
now again. I fly through time zones to my tomorrow,
leave you in my yesterday.

Let the song lines be sung always, full of
musings, memories and absences. Let the dark
always give way to light. Let me come back
again and again

to stand with you in another tomorrow under
a blue Brisbane sky, wonder at the beauty
of this land and hold in memory transient
moments of your life.

Skylark

She dreamed she could fly, in the happy
days of her short life.

On this day and on the tomorrows we
live without her, I will marvel at her
courage and the surge of her life force
which lifted her up and up beyond
our reach.

I will remember her when I hear
the song of the skylark, and wonder
causes me to gasp on an intake of
the breath which left her anchored
body and set her free.

The Air I Breathe

The air I breathe is the raging wind
of the tsunami, the gentle summer
breeze, the billow blowing through
washed sheets, the trill of a songbird,
the roar of a savage, the gasp of a
victim, the cry of a newborn, the peal
of children's laughter, a lover's sigh,
a widow's groan, the scent of a garden.

It is the first and last breath you breathed.
I inhale, exhale, all that is, was and will be.
My last breath will be your breath and her
breath and his breath and their breath taken,
given, from fish, bird, mammoth, insect,
saint, sinner, builder, destroyer, wise, foolish;

filtered, renewed in the verdant growth
of rainforest, fresh in the ozone of oceans
surging under the moon's desire.
I breathe the joy, the sorrow, and accept
all that is, was and will be; the glory
you surrendered to with your dying breath.

I Am

I am fear, anxiety, courage, hope,
dread, sorrow, innocence, joy.

Mishmashed, pummelled, pounded,
tang-tasted, salted, spooned, cooked,
crumbled, blended, broken, flattened,
flipped, grated, gobbled.

I am in all things sighted, glimpsed,
heard, touched, tongued, past, present,
lost, found, transient, permanent, dead,
dormant.

I am again and again, birthing, becoming,
behind, before, beyond. I am.